BLOOD RED

BLOOD RED

Poems by

Barbara Schlichting

Blood Red

Copyright 2019 © Barbara Schlichting
All Rights Reserved

Formatting – Wild Seas Formatting
www.WildSeasFormatting.com

Published by First Lady Press
Bemidji, MN 56601 http://www.barbaraschlichting.com

ISBN 978-1-7324308-8-4

For my family,

For my friends,

Enjoy these books by Barbara Schlichting

Picture Books
By Barbie Marie

Martha Washington: HER FIRST FEW DAYS AS FIRST LADY

Red Shoes

Poetry
WHISPERS FROM THE WIND

BLOOD RED

By Barbara Schlichting

Single Titles
THE BROKEN CIRCLE

First Ladies Mystery Series
Dolley Madison: THE BLOOD SPANGLED BANNER

Mary Lincoln: IF WORDS COULD KILL

Edith Wilson: THE CLUE OF THE DANCING BELL

A WHITE HOUSE DOLLHOUSE MYSTERY
Edith Wilson: FOURTEEN POINTS to DEATH

HISTORICAL FICTION
BODY ON THE TRACKS

Table of contents

Enjoy these books by Barbara Schlichting	8
Table of contents	10
Home and Family	1
Blood Red	2
Grandpa	3
Friends Forever	4
Drinking Friends	5
How Do You Know?	6
The New Bathing Suit	7
The New Person	8
Here We Go Again	9
Two Shots	10
The Kiss	11
They Disappeared	12
How Are You?	13
She Will Be Here	15
Love	17
Up, Up, Up	19
Love is in The Air	21
Where Will We Be?	22
Once More	23
Holding Hands	24
Smiling at the Sun	25
Beautiful	26
Ice Cream	27
We Are Growing	28
She is Here	29
Down to Earth	30
Let's Go	31
The Sun	32
Same as Me	33

Songs of Solace	35
Songs of Silence	36
From the Start	37
The Memory	38
Tonight or is it Today?	39
So There	40
Alone Together	41
When Will We Begin	42
Once Upon a Time	43
All Things Considered	45
Tall, Dark, and Handsome	47
Playing in the Sun	48
The Clothesline	50
Cancer	51
Go Blow	52
Mom's	53
Mixing Bowls	54
Women and Friends	55
Roll the Ball	56
Grandchildren	57
Birthday Cake	58
My First Love	59
Dad	60
Chuckling	61
Sunflower	62
Moon	63
The Grass	64
The Chair	65
My Mother's Voice	66
Washing Hair	67
Dresses	68
Bacon and Eggs	69
The End	70

Home and Family

The Clothesline
Cancer
Go Blow
Mom's
Mixing Bowls
Women and Friends
Roll the Ball
Grandchildren
Birthday Cake
My First Love
Dad
Chuckling
Sunflower
Moon
The Grass
The Chair
My Mother's Voice
Washing Hair
Dresses
Bacon and Eggs
The End

Blood Red

Pumping
through my veins and into my soul
inching it away

My soul awaits
my spirit is ageless
my fingers reach out to alert my soul
but it's only a whisper in the wind and nothing more

My toes touch the floor,
the earth below rises up to meet my soul
my spirit
but it's unwelcome

The blood red crackles outside my heart and into the abyss
feathering and fondling what grows inside
because my lady love will
soon join me.

My life has past
I am in the Eternity.

Grandpa

The six-foot, blue eyed Swede
stood next to his locomotive,
holding a small hand

The brown-eyed, blonde little girl
with a pony tail,
wrapped her arms around her grandpa's neck

He looked at his pocket watch,
then nodded to the conductor
and switchman

He handed the little girl to his son,
before kissing the top of
granddaughter's head
Goodbye.

Friends Forever

Friends forever

Friends for life

Friends to skip rope with

Friends to hang out
and watch the boys go by with

Friends to believe in

Friends to find hope with

Friends to grow up
and become adults with

Friends to grow old with and

Friends to die with.

Drinking Friends

Onward and upward
   We go
Over the land
   And out the door.

Over and under
    Each other's hearts

Until the will
   To live
Has passed us by

Then
We say

Goodbye

How Do You Know?

The earth is brown
And green

My sweetheart's eyes
Are blue.

I miss his smile
That lit his eyes
Every time he'd see me.

I wonder
When I'll see him?

Will my eyes
Light the sky
when they see his?

How do you know if the sun
Rises and falls

Or the moon sets
Over him?
Or us?

Someday,
The day will come

And,
Then we'll know.

The New Bathing Suit

The elastic is tight
suppressing the wrinkled skin.
The bust is flat
without noticeable cleavage.
The excess belly fat is tucked in
 like a tight bowtie.
The thighs cling together
 like an elephant's eye.
The legs are too white
 and will blind an ostrich.
The rear end is lumpy
like a bowl of popped popcorn.

Why did I look in the mirror?

The New Person

Will he notice the scar on my back?

The deep dark one that crosses from my shoulder blade to under my armpit?

What will he say?

"Will it go away?"

"No. It'll be like that forever and ever."

"What about more lotion?"

"No. It'll only become darker over time."

"Oh."

What will he say about all the stretchmarks that criss-cross my lily white skin like a roadmap.

"I suppose the marks are from babies?"

"Yes."

"Will they go away?"

"No."

"With lotion?"

"No."

What will happen when I stay in the shade?

Will he say, "You need to be in the sun? You need color?"

"No!" I'll say. "I have skin cancer constantly."

"So!" he'll say, "cover up."

"No! I don't want melanoma again."

"You need sun. You're too white!"

"See you," I say.

And leave.

Here We Go Again

Up and down
again

You see her
But not me

You are tall, muscular
Me, I'm petite

When will you see
me?

Today or tomorrow?

In the morning at the coffee pot?
In the early afternoon at the copy machine?
In the late afternoon at the elevator?

She'll go her separate way
without saying good night,

but, I will.

Tomorrow morning,
we'll go up and down
again.

Two Shots

Straight up

It's summer and dishes are done
the kitchen cleaned.

I'm ready to flirt and dance and shake my hips,
let's get the invites going.

I'll get the bottle from
behind the bed
and the smokes hidden
behind the socks where Mom doesn't look.

The party starts when they leave,
Mom and Dad.

Baby brother is with Grandma.
Big brother is away for the weekend.

It's time to party.

The Kiss

Some are hot like the sun
with strong rays
that knock off my socks
leaving my feet hot.

A kiss
will leave me hot
all the way down to my toes
which are on fire.
A sun kiss will dimple my cheeks
and make me hot.

The top of my head is hot
and sweaty from the sun.
My hair feels hot
his kisses.

Is it because of his kiss or the sun that I feel so hot?
Is it possible to charge a pair of lips?
Did he pump me up with a battery?
He must've put his lips into a socket
which charged my battery.

Or is the sun charging me up like a ripe tomato?

They Disappeared

The color is white
The color is black
The colors mesh into the night
The people run
To who knows were
But find some freedom
From the newborn air

The sky is blue
The sky is black

The morning brings
Anew

The heavens open
And make things right

The colors become
White, black, red and brown
The new color form
Anew
And make a one.

How Are You?

Where are we?
I've missed you since you went away
to War
You returned
but not the same
So you told me
I didn't understand
because I was so young
so were you
but I've always been lonesome for you
I followed what you requested
I met another
and started a new life
without you.
Are you ever lonesome for me?
Do you think of me?

It's here, you know
it's here
Right in the heart
where it hurts
stuck
piercing my veins and memory arteries
the arrow
It don't bleed anymore
except the love
which continues to seep out

through the threads and into my soul

What happened?
Will you ever tell me?
I think that you will
but you won't.
Did you leave
for another woman
or had you lost your love
for me?
I do not know.

And now I'm stuck
without you.

You're up there
in Heaven
whispering in my ear
telling me that your arms are unfurled
and waiting to hold me
once again
when I meet you once again.

She Will Be Here

I know she will be here
when she can.
My woman
who I once held in my arms
and once promised a life
so I wait.

I follow her along
all day
just like a puppy dog
wagging its tail.
I think she knows that I'm here,
along beside her
throughout the long day.

Was that my name whispered
when we passed the old church
where we should've been married?
Instead someone else
took her hand
and led the way.

But her heart remembers my name
in the dark
when her eyes are closed
when light cannot see
how her heart flows just for me
for in her dreams

she says my name

Beloved
when I do hers
Dearest
the time will come
and we will be one
when she no longer walks the earth.

Love

We are here
Loving each other
In an odd way

You're up above
Watching me walk
Hearing me talk
But I can't see you
Walk
Or talk.

Sometimes
I feel your spirit near
Sometimes
I hear words
In my ears
Which were private
Between you and I
That's why I know it's you.

Sometimes
I pretend
That we are
Dancing, swaying
Like before
That you are holding me tight
And loving me.

Like before

I cannot wait
For my death
Because you are
Below the earth
Looking down
At my earth
Where I walk
Live
Sing and sway
While dreaming
About you.

Up, Up, Up

He says to me
every morning
when he reaches down
to lightly trace
my jawline
nose
neck
He's with the Angels
so I'm unaware
of his touch
I say, "Okay. You're right. It's time."
I get up and dress
still yawning
and meet the day
with my routine
of him by my side
guiding my footsteps
Tell me it's best to do the laundry today
tomorrow it'll rain
Bake cookies or a cake
in case a friend stops to visit
So I do
It does rain
Two friends stop in for coffee and treats
Later,
I think,
we will meet

with the Angels singing
and I will thank him
for all of his good advice
with a kiss.

Love is in The Air

But, I'm down here
where the birds chirp
And you are everywhere
where the cherubs sing
You are not with me
yet I wonder
are you safe
warm
well-fed up above?

I know it sounds stupid
but how do I know
since I can't
hear the cherubs sing,
only hear
Your favorite bird
the Robin
Sing

Where Will We Be?

Will we meet in the garden?
while I tend my flowers
of roses, tulips, and daffodils
Or will it be in bed
between the soft sheets
and on top of my comfortable mattress?

Then I'll reach out my arms
And say, "Honey, I'm coming home to you, I'm almost with you."
And my husband will say, "Sweetheart, you're almost home."
I'll say, "I want your arms around me."

And you will
When that sweet dark night,
Arrives.

Once More

We will hold hands and walk
step on each other's toes
by each other's side
until the end of time.

We will go
once more until we can look into each other's eyes
from the side of the moon
and see the stars.

See our star
points emblazoned
I LUV U

Which awaits
Us Two
where we will sit once more
Beside each other
Sharing our breath
As One.

Holding Hands

Your left hand takes my right,
it feels right.
Although,
when you hold it tight
my toes turn bright.
The idea of your hand holding mine tight
sends bright
spheres to my tights.
My tights get too tight
and then I want to
be loose.
So I make myself loose
and take off the tights.
But then,
your left hand takes my right,
and my underwear feels tight.
So I remove them — anything that makes me feel tight.
Now it's my birthday suit but I don't feel tight anymore
because the sheet covering us
leaves us bare
and exposed
to the bright moon light.

Smiling at the Sun

The sun
smiles aglow.

When will you — my love,
take my hand
and never it let it go — again.

My man is all around
and aglow
with love.

I feel it in his eyes
they are filled with the sun.

His nose twinkles with twitches,
when he leans in closer
for more kisses.

Now my eyes turn toward the sun
and think of his bright blue eyes
and the way he made me feel — back then
when he walked the green grass and held my shaky hand.

Now, he keeps the sun in my eyes,
he holds me to the light
so he can always see me, but I only see the sun.

Now we wait until we can see each other
and hold our hands — once again as lovers.

Beautiful

Are the ravens when they speak
Nevermore

Beautiful was the morning sun, when it shone in your eyes
Nevermore

Beautiful was your radiant smile when it met mine
Nevermore

Beautiful was your passionate kiss when your lips met mine
Nevermore

We will meet once again when the comforting earth demands

And the earth will embrace our souls because you'll be beside me
Once again.

Ice Cream

It melts all over

Chocolate, strawberry, banana, peppermint
and cherry.

Your fingers are
Brown, red, pink, yellow, rose, and striped.

Your tongue is
Lavender, mauve, black and blue

But you don't see it until you stick your tongue out at mirror,
then laugh.

Until you're ready for another
round of chocolate, strawberry, banana, peppermint
and cherry.

Which makes your tongue
quite merry
 and you're quite jolly.

We Are Growing

We grow together
From soft voices
In the night.

We grow together
Old
With the Earth.

We grow together
With passion
In each other's arms
Where we learn to love
Without seeing or feeling
Except through memory threads
Of our Flesh
Still Hot from the Threads.

Knowing the other is there
Holding us up
Till we will meet once again
And continue our threads
With new memories.

She is Here

I watch from Heaven
For my long ago love
She is here
red hair blazing
from afar
Sweet smile
reminds me of strawberries
There she is
Beneath my feet.

She walks
under the blue sky
which was the color of my lover's eyes
when he told me
my hair blazed red
my lips tasted like strawberries
But I know
when he looks down and sings me to sleep
Because
my soul is calm
and I am complete.

Down to Earth

We will walk the Earth
you and I
Alone with our smiles
and our hearts
Together our hands fold
clutching
Then we can sing
Bridge Over Troubled Water
to the wind
and softly whisper
our lover's name
as one.

Let's Go

To the sea
To the sea
To him
He left you behind
Because of the war
Because of his changing mind
He left you behind
Go
Be together
Once more
In the sea.

The Sun

The sun shines bright
and so do you.

Our love is brighter
but I cannot see you.

Your light is brighter
it shines on me
And my light brightens you
even though you're in the sky.

We hold each other up
to the light.

Same as Me

Letting go
for the future.
Must I look ahead
into the spell of the beyond?

If I do go into the future
without you
I won't be letting go
because you are the same as me
our hopes
dreams
are the same.

I won't be letting go
because we are the same.

Our mothers knew each other
before this life
and promised us our
future together
because we are the same.

Have many children
we promised each other.
We vowed to love one another
to be a good mother and father
raise a family
make our parents proud.

But it wasn't meant to be
now we wait
until we can be together again
in another lifetime
and we can make our new parents proud
we must wait for the time to come
but we are
one in the same.

Songs of Solace

Fill my being
with comfort
Fill my heart
with love
Fill my soul
with you

A shelter
to the Soul
Heart
and Being.

Songs of Silence

Songs of silence

the air is void

my ears are open

waiting to hear your sweet voice

but you

fill my heart

as I wait

for your homecoming

which will be

my homecoming.

From the Start

What do we say
to one another
whn it's goodbye?

tears sting
my red nose hurts
let's talk about old times
memories that we can't forget
because they're strong and true

but goodbye to you
I wish you well
joy and happiness.

For goodbye isn't forever
because love is
and we have our journeys.

So goodbye
peace be with you
on life's journey
my friend and lover.

I say we say goodbye
with a handshake and a nod
and walk to our life
and make it our own.

The Memory

The tree stands alone
its branches
bend and flow with the gushing wind
where the leaves sway and scratch against her window
saying the distant name
of her once beloved
she knows that it's him
because his voice belongs to her.

The memory calls to her
in the night when she lays sleeping
and dreaming about loves sweet sorrows.

Waking, she knows that He's with her
like the strong oak outside the window.

She wishes to be with her long ago lover
but the branches haven't withered
for it's not her time,
but her man stays with her
strong and true like the might oak
leading her through her tomorrows.

Tonight or is it Today?

I sit by the window and see the clouds drift overhead
puffy and white.
The woman beside me looks much the same
still
her jaw is open
but she licks her teeth
sudden and soundless
When will the end come?
On the bedstead are a few books
several children's
Harper Lee
Or the Shot Heard Round the World and the American Revolution.

Which should I read next
the longest or the shortest?
I picked up the children's picture book
and read it aloud.

She shut her eyes,
and remembered
green eggs tasted normal,
she's sure the little engine made it to the top
and the ducklings made it across the street.
She smiled.

So There

Off we go
to the sea
over the hills
over the mountains
toward the end
of the world
where I'll be
wrapped in the light of
the center
of my mother's arms
all the more.

Alone Together

There are you
sitting straight and tall
tired
lonesome
fearful
reading the paper
ignoring me.
But I feel alone.
There you are
watching TV
embracing the remote control
instead of me.

We are alone,
together.

When Will We Begin

to understand each other?
Do you see the bright sunshine
when I pass by?

The sky is dark gray
I hold out the umbrella
but you turn away.

When I fall
will you pick me up
or feed me
when my belly aches?

Or my shoes are washed away and all that's left is pain?

Once Upon a Time

there was a girl
far away
who held fast to her heart
but it ached so for her love
who lived beyond her fingertips
out in the universe
never to be seen again
but then he appeared in a dream
he looked so real
standing tall and proud in his uniform
a proud Marine
just like she remembered but
why in a dream?
Where was he?
Why appear this way to her?
Then she found the old pictures and shut her eyes.
She pictured them laughing and dancing and smiling
in each other's arms
her head on his shoulder
and his on hers
as he held her tight
she didn't want to see him go
she watched him march to war.

his gentle spirit
caring nature
warm kisses

kindness
soft spoken nature
firm in their love
commitment
gone.

his mind
taken
by seeing too much
killing too much
loss of too many comrades
in a foreign land
Vietnam.

He never saw goodness again.
Nor did she see him.

All Things Considered

we are here
then and now
is it a warning
that it'll be tough each
morning
evening
night
with you up above guiding my footsteps
without me knowing
and me
walking the Earth
alone
backwards and forward
up and down
in and out
not knowing you are my inner spirit.

We are out of order,
you and I
but
we choose our way
together
as strangers re we
threading our past
with our future.

Till death do us part

they say
or is it
till we join
and envelope each other forever after?
for time does not exist
where we will lay with our arms entwined
and legs tangled
dance across the dark sky
and see the light in each other's eyes?

The Forevermore
will give us a new life
where we will sing and dance
and love across the twinkling star lights.

Tall, Dark, and Handsome

There he is walking through the door
Tall, dark, and handsome.

She is tall, fair, and blonde

He holds her hand, and squeezes it.

She swishes and sways her skirts like the
Rocky Mountain hummingbird.

His heart beats like the red hummingbird
outside the window.

The red hummingbird sees the Rocky Mountain skirts.

He is tall, dark, and handsome
She is tall, fair, and blonde.

Together they dance

Playing in the Sun

It's snowing
It's blowing
It's sunning
It's shining

We can go ski-doing
We can go sledding
We can go waterskiing
And swimming

My swimsuit says
To stay home

My snowsuit says
It's a go.

The Clothesline

It's way over my head as I pin the sheets onto the line
There's room for the pink towels and the blue.

We had twins.
A boy and a girl.

Now, what do I do?

As I pin the sheets to dry,
And hang the diapers, which my mother made for me since they're cheaper than purchasing them, I think of when I wanted a child.
But my friend had three. That would be crazier than two, wouldn't it? My mom says, 'it'll get easier when they get bigger.' I'm sure that she's right. I'm glad that the two are happy and healthy. What else could you ask for?

A full-night's sleep.
A bathroom that doesn't stink all the time.
A day without washing diapers.
A full, uninterrupted fifteen-minute coffee break. One that I can drink a hot cup of coffee all at once. And drink it with a warm chocolate-chip cookie. My favorite.

But, my hubby still tells me I'm beautiful.
I shouldn't ask for anything more.

Cancer

Where are you?

You're here and there and everywhere.

You're hidden in my vagina,

skin, and parts unknown—yet.

There's also HPV and PAP tests.

I better not find you in my breasts like what happened to my girlfriend who quit having her breasts squeezed because it was too painful. She quit having a yearly PAP test. She quit being screened. They all caused cancer, in her eyes.

My girlfriend who'd had breast cancer and partial mastectomy, told me,

No more mammograms. The stress causes cancer.

No more PAP test, either. She won't spread her legs anymore for anyone or for anything.

She died from throat cancer.

Go figure.

Does this make sense?

Go Blow

Blow your nose
Blow your hair
Blow your toes

Blow out your gum
then you can hum

Blow out the corn
in your ears
so you can hear!

Don't ya want to hear!
Quit shouting!

Wipe your nose
it's dripping.

Your hair
needs trimming
you look like a bum.

Your toes are all dirty.
You washed them and blew on them
but they are all dirty.

Use clean water from the house this time
Don't wash in the creeks.

They are all dirty!

Mom's

Mother was warm and fuzzy

She wore a fuzzy robe and distinctive smile, like she had something up her sleeve. She usually did.

She smiled when she saw me

As a young woman, mother — growing older like her.

She loved my children — two boys.

Her grandchildren.

The boys, caught a snapping turtle once when we visited her.

The next visit, we ate turtle soup. First she told us it was chicken, then confessed it was turtle when the bowls were clean.

She sneaked green tomato pie one day onto the table and I liked it.

Before that, I told her never to serve green tomato pie to me because I knew I'd hate it.

First son raised chickens and named them. I never told him which one we stuffed and roasted for Sunday dinner. Second son wanted to play the drums so I gave him piano lessons instead.

Mixing Bowls

It was passed down to me.
Her bowls.
The bowls that she'd mix
cakes, cookies, donuts,
eggs, and all sorts of things in
plus Jell-o.

I set the stacked bowls
up high,
not intending to use them
because they were hers.

I didn't want to risk breaking them,
either.
The memory of her mixing,
turning the spatula
and pouring the batter out,
was too strong.

I found a recipe.
Just like one she'd made. That favored chocolate cake.
Mixed it up and baked it.

Washed the bowl.
Put it back on the shelf in its correct place.
Now the bowl is mine.
Will my daughter make it hers?

Women and Friends

It takes all kinds
to make the world go round
but,
my girlfriends are special.
There's one friend
that will listen to me gripe about my husband
and another to gripe about my kids.
Then there's this other friend who listen to me gripe about my older brother.
However,
I sing praises too.
About my brother, the other one,
and sometimes the older one.
My mother was good to me in so many ways
and so was Dad.
There's friends that will listen when I've discovered news about
my great-grandpa and grandma.
They think it's interesting.
So, dearest of friends,
Thanks be to God and all of you
for keeping me sane and grounded.
My feet are planted.
I'll listen to all of yours gripes, whenever you want me to.
Thanks.

Roll the Ball

He wants to play, too.

He doesn't see well.

Nor does he have the coordination because of cerebral palsy.

But he likes to roll the basketball on the playground during recess.

His legs fold up underneath as he lowers himself to the pavement, letting his crutches land near him. Then he waits for a friend to fetch a ball. The friend is reluctant to sit on the ground because the pavement is cold and wet, but does. The ball is passed back and forth until the bell rings indicating the end of recess.

The friend extends his arms, and hands over the crutches, allowing the boy to lean on him for balance. The friend carries the ball as they follow indoors with the other classmates.

Who will roll it to the boy who isn't like us?

Grandchildren

Grandchildren make us feel young again.

Then, I hear, that we're not to think of ourselves as old.

I must be old since I have grandchildren in their twenties.

So what are these people talking about? I am old.

I am old enough to enjoy taking my granddaughter to see different Laura Ingalls Wilder sites. She loved it. We got to know each other better. We talked about school and her favorite clothes, colors and ice cream flavors.

I am old enough to enjoy my grandson, too. He brought me to a movie before he left for his three-year stint in the army. I also go to hockey games and know what some of the terms mean like 'hat trick', and 'butterfly' goalie saves.

With my kids, I learned along the way but still had to discipline. Now, I don't. I can offer them ice cream before they go to sleep. I can keep them up and play games and not worry about how tired they'll be in the morning. If the diapers were dirty or someone got a belly ache, it wasn't my problem. Mom and Dad could take of the situation.

Yes, I am older or old. I'm old enough to enjoy my grandchildren and young enough to know that the parents will take care of the discipline because it's not my job.

My job is to love them.

Birthday Cake

I want chocolate.
You'll get what I bake.
It's my birthday
Grandma and Grandpa don't like chocolate
I do and it's my birthday
They're you're grandparents, show respect
Well, okay, but I can still want chocolate
Yes, you can still want it but that doesn't mean you'll get it.
Yes, Mother.
It's naptime.

I closed my eyes and dreamed and when I woke, I took a deep breath. My lungs filled with the lovely smell of fresh cake and brewed coffee.

Familiar voices from the livingroom rose and fell, telling me that the grandparents I needed to show respect for, were here.

In the livingroom, their eyes sparkled as they smiled upon me.

I blew out three candles and then we ate white cake with chocolate frosting and vanilla ice cream.

My First Love

She gazed upon me
And smiled.
She counted my fingers and toes
And smiled.
She made sure the diapers were pinned just right
And smiled.
She fed me
And smiled
She softly whispered and sang good night to me
And smiled.

I gurgled.
And smiled at her.
I played with my fingers and toes
And smiled at her.
I squirmed when she fastened the diapers
And smiled at her.
I cooed when she filled my belly
And smiled.
Her voice caused me to
Smile.

Mom.

Dad

Dad held me high
and sighed
Dad tickled me
and made me giggle
We snuggled
and squirmed together
when I sat on his lap.
His lap was made for me to sit on
but he wiggled because my ponytail made
his nose twitch.

We giggled and chuckled together
Went for strawberry and me chocolate, ice cream cones.
We drove around town
We'd stop and watch the planes fly overhead.
We'd go to the Union Depot and look at the trains
We'd talk about the good old days when his dad was an engineer for the Milwaukee Railroad.

I miss our talks about his parents
Growing up
When we went for Sunday drives when I was little and my brothers were, too.
Now, I talk about my parents with my grandkids
Who really don't care.

Hopefully, they will someday.

Chuckling
Giggling
Kissing
Hugging
Loving
Rolling
Together

Sunflower

On my shoulder
Sunflower
In my eyes
Make me glow
Like a globe

Moon

The moon feathers
The snow like a winter's brush
Of diamonds and sparkles and
Twinkles onto the deep snow
The white snow is powdery and soft
But crunches down deep underfoot
My knee-high boots
Carry me far deeper into the woods
Where only the moon
Sees me

The Grass

The green grass and colorful flowers
Of red, purple, yellow, and blue
Brighten the sky, my eyes and the floor I walk on.
The radiant colors of the blue sky
Cause the bright green grass to become brighter, and fashionable
Like a parade.
In a line, like preschool children, all the reds, purples, and shades of yellows Flowers line up
And march before me, like a parade,
Into fall.
The green tree leaves
Become orange and red
The preschool row curls up, and learn to hold hands,
They are ready for kindergarten
And spring.

The Chair

It belongs to him
I don't sit on it.
No one does.
He naps
Turns the TV stations
And plays games on his laptop

I have my own chair
It belongs to me and family
I write letters
Read books
Talk to grandchildren
Plan the day
Drink coffee
And dream of tomorrow

My Mother's Voice

Her voice was distinctive.
It resonated in my head
and bounced from ear to ear
within my head.

I could tell when she was mad
and wanted to throw me into the zoo
or the garbage can.

I'm sure she wanted to throw me into the garbage can
when I didn't want to wash dishes and threw the dishes into the garbage can.

Then my mother became older.
Her voice became shallow, but her eyes were still bright.
She'd see me and her eyes lit mine like a child.

She owned me.
Now I own her.

Washing Hair

She brought the kitchen chair to the sink,
The one with the tallest back.
She placed the thick phone directory on top
Then motioned for me to climb up and kneel on it.
So I did.

She wrapped the large bathroom towel around my neck and pinned it tight.
I almost couldn't breathe.
She folded towels and placed them on the counterspace between the sink and me.
I leaned forward.
Mom moistened my hair and scrubbed it clean.
She flipped the towel over my head when finished to dry my hair.

She combed my blonde hair and clipped the sides back with a barrett.
She lifted me down.

I went to play.

Dresses

The wrinkles
Lay on the counter
They crinkle
While she cuts
The fabric
Glistens and listens
To the scissors
As they clip
And snip
Patch
and sew
Dresses

Bacon and Eggs

Toast and butter
Jam and peanut butter
Scrambled eggs and bacon
Pancakes and syrup
Waffles and syrup
Toast and strawberry jelly
Apple jelly and apple sauce
They all go together
Like a morning weekend treat
Where we seat ourselves
Beside our treat — family

The End
Is just the beginning
Which brings us
To the middle
The middle
Brings us the beginning
Of the middle
Of the end
Then it's
The end.

www.ingramcontent.com/pod-product-compliance
Lightning Source LLC
Chambersburg PA
CBHW052113070526
44584CB00017B/2461